CHRISTIANITY CRU

BY

HENRY BURR, Ph.D., Sc.D.

AND

MARGUERITE BEIGHTON PLESS, D.D.

PUBLISHED BY
THE BERT ROSE COMPANY
Los Angeles, California

Kessinger Publishing's Rare Reprints
Thousands of Scarce and Hard-to-Find Books!

· · ·
· · ·
· · ·
· · ·
· · ·
· · ·
· · ·
· · ·
· · ·
· · ·
· · ·
· · ·
· · ·
· · ·
· · ·
· · ·
· · ·
· · ·
· · ·

HENRY BURR, Ph.D.Sc.D.

MARGUERITE BEIGHTON PLESS

FOREWORD

Our purpose in writing this book is to bring before the public in as brief and intelligible form as possible, the true knowledge and information concerning Christianity. One difficulty in achieving this has been to condense in one short book what really requires several volumes for expression.

The word "Reincarnation" as used in the following chapters, is at all times to be construed as meaning part of the true Christianity of Christ. Its definition is: "the spiritual evolution of the Soul, emanating from God, and passing through all necessary forms of expression in many different lives, until the attainment of conscious unity with God—"My Father and your Father."

The Christian concept of Reincarnation is therefore far removed from Buddhism and the Theosophist thought, which merely embody cold scientific principles. On the contrary, Christian Reincarnation is a **religion,** based on active worship of God, the Father as revealed by Christ.

The authors will be pleased at all times to answer through the publishers any questions pertaining to the facts, historical or otherwise, herein stated.

INDEX

Chapter I - - - - - THE ANCIENT CORNER-STONE

Chapter II - - - - CHRIST, THE REINCARNATIONIST

Chapter III - - - - - - - EARLY CHRISTIANITY

Chapter IV - - - - - - - - - - CRUCIFIXION

Chapter V - - - - - - - - - - RESURRECTION

Chapter VI - - - - - - - - - SHIFTING SANDS

Chapter VII - - - - - - - - THE BETTER DAWN

INTRODUCTION

"By their fruits ye shall know them," and by world conditions today, Christianity must stand to be judged after nineteen centuries.

What vital element is lacking? What travesty of the teachings of Christ Who came to bring "Peace on earth," Who said, "Love one another," and "Be ye therefore perfect," has permitted the terrific world upheaval that now confronts us?

In bacterial diseases, a microscopic examination is necessary to ascertain the cause, before a diagnosis can be made and a remedy prescribed.

Reasoning thus, we have earnestly sought to discover what has produced the diseased spiritual condition manifest among many professing Christians, and the reason why so many have retrogressed into the chronic state of atheism and agnosticism.

In the resultant search that has led to all sources of the oldest known beliefs, and to the cradle of Christianity itself, startling truths have been discovered. By a keen survey of historical FACTS connected with religion, philosophy, and science, the divergence of the Christian Churches from the true teachings of Christ has been traced from its outset. This disobedience to high spiritual law has produced as an inevitable result, the disease and corruption inherent in the religion of today: **a re-ligion of Fear and Injustice,** binding man down with the chains of "original sin" in direct contravention of the words of Christ.

The people have grown weary of the wrathful, destructive Jehovah of the Old Testament—a God made in the image of man. They turn back the pages of history and find them stained crimson with innocent blood shed in the name of false Christianity. The horrors of the World War are still vivid in their minds; they cry aloud in their fear and scornful doubt, "Is there a God, after all?"

The rapid progress of Science adds to the chaos of doubt and scepticism. The old conception of the universe is changed; what was once regarded as merely "dead matter" is now conceived as ever-mobile creative energy. The Yahweh of the ancient Jews, still worshipped instead of the God of Christ, no longer fits into the modern picture.

> "He saw the boundless scheme dilate,
> In star and blossom, sky and clod,
> And as the universe grew great,
> He dreamed for it a greater God."

The structure of Christianity, built on the false concept and theology of man, totters under the impact of each new scientific discovery. The young people especially, turn away from the churches; religion cannot answer their insistent questions. They are told to have faith, to deny the evidence of their God-given intelligence.

Yet Truth never conflicts with Truth! Why have the pathways of Science and Christianity so diverged that the thinker must choose between them?

A building is no stronger than its foundation; if the corner-stone is removed the whole structure is endangered. Buried deep under the fast-accumulating wreckage of the failing structure of Christianity, lies the rejected corner-stone, overthrown by the intolerance and greed for temporal power of certain of the leaders of the early church; upheld staunchly by others—the founders of true Christian theology, but collapsing at last in rivers of blood, the martyr blood of the real Christians who died fighting to save it from destruction.

This Corner-Stone of TRUE CHRISTIANITY as taught by Christ is the belief in REINCARNATION!

Without its support the teachings of Christ become meaningless, robbed of their true import and spiritual essence; the fallacies of man creep in, false gods arise. The inevitable parting of the ways must come; Science, following ever the pathway of Truth, can no longer travel hand-in-hand with this Christianity that is not of Christ but of man.

Herein lies the cause of the spiritual disease of today. The grim specter of Injustice that stalks the earth, destroying all hope for suffering humanity is a product of this rejection of the truth of Reincarnation, leading to the worship of the ancient Jewish tribal God of injustice, wrath, and destruction—the despotic Yahweh set up as a graven image instead of the true God revealed by Christ. Had the early Church followed the teachings of Christ the Reincarnationist instead of Judaism interspersed with such false interpretations as would continue to hold the people in fear and subjection, the world would have advanced beyond the possibility of such conditions as exist today.

This is our sincere and final diagnosis after exhaustive investigation and most painstaking and complete analysis of all conditions involved. Our report, based on the findings of FACTS, follows in the succeeding chapters, for the examination and unbiased consideration of all thinkers in search of Truth.

CHAPTER I.

THE ANCIENT CORNER-STONE

Whether we travel along the banks of the White Nile or the Blue Nile, past the six cataracts and into the heart of Africa, or follow the yellow waters of the Ganges up into the jungles of Asia, the earliest records known to man, establish clearly the belief in Reincarnation as ever-existant.

Even earlier than 5000 B. C. the Caucasian inhabitants of Egypt had a very advanced civilization. The first historically fixed date known to man was established there in 4241 B. C. through the creation of the calendar year. In that land of unsurpassed climate, the largest of the famous Pyramids was built five hundred years later. There also during the early periods, the Great Sphinx symbol of Harmachis — "morning sun" — was erected. This enormous figure carved in rock, eternally gazes with brooding, inscrutable eyes over the vast reaches of desert sand in the shadow of the Pyramids, its recumbent attitude exactly similar to that assumed by the larva of the hawk-moth, or "Sphingidae," the pose forever symbolic of Reincarnation—the earth-bound crawling worm lifting its head from the mud, in the urge toward the glorious transformation that shall bear it upward in the winged flight of freedom.

In this ancient land in the 15th century B. C. King Thutmose III, ruled, rising from priesthood into the position of a general, greater and more advanced than either Alexander, Caesar, or Napoleon were later. This was long before the first Biblical records were made, and it can be confidently admitted with Herodotus—most reliable of the early Greek writers—that the Egyptians were the original teachers of re-birth. There is substantial evidence of this fact in archaelogical discoveries showing that many centuries before Moses, the priests of old Egypt taught the passing of the Soul —BA—through different bodies, after crossing YARU, since then mis-named death.*

In the early days of China where historical records date back to only twenty-five centuries B. C., the belief in Reincarnation was also taught there by the great philosophers Lav-Tze and Chaang-Tze. The same belief is recorded in Central Asia under one aspect or another as far back as can be traced, till one is confronted with the first

_____

*BA (often mis-named KA) means the Soul; KA means only the higher intelligence, or "genius" of the body.

periods, as impenetrable as the jungle fastness.

In India, where the Vedic religion followed the Aryan invasion, and is traced back to about 1500 B. C. at a time when Egypt had known many secular glories, Buddhism came into being at the comparatively recent period of the sixth century B. C. Its great influence over Asia is well-known. There has been some discussion among scholars as to its origin, but all evidence tends to prove that it branched off from Egyptian teachings on the foundation of re-birth.

Before the advent of Buddhism, the Magi of Persia and Chaldea in the East had also branched off from the same Egyptian tree of knowledge. This is shown definitely by their scientific foundation, similar to that of the builders of the Pyramids, and proven also by their belief in re-birth.

Oldest antiquity shows us therefore, a practically universal creed: that of Reincarnation; the trail blazed through the ages by man's deep spiritual intuition and sense of potential divinity and immortality, leading to the mountain-top of Truth.

Our own investigation, not only in Egypt, but throughout Africa and other continents, has revealed the same belief to have been ever-present. It has appeared to be as vivid with tribes remained primitive as it was with the Masters of all knowledge in the earliest periods.

As far back as can be historically established, Egypt ruled supreme through her priests, in the fields of Science. Centers such as Heliopolis drew all, from near and far, in search of knowledge. Moses was unquestionably initiated in one or more of these centers, and gained there his legislative knowledge. The similarity between the laws of the great Hebrew concerning Justice and Right, and the early maxims of Ptah-Hotep and other Egyptian teachers, amply corroborates this viewpoint. Compared with the ancient Egyptians, the Israelites were a young race, historically speaking, since the first records related to them date back only to 1225 B. C.*

A striking indication of the Egyptian influence on the former desert tribes of Israel, roaming side by side with the Bedouins, is manifested in the principal function of the first Hebrew priests— that of Divination by Art. We know also that the symbolism of the serpent—so vivid throughout the Old Testament—originated in the early Egyptian

---

* It was only recently discovered that the Book of Proverbs comes from Egyptian sources, as proven by the translation of the Egyptian teachings of Amenophis, the son of Kanakht.

temples. Those who have visited the African section of the mysterious Timbuctoo, know how strongly this same symbolism still holds sway. Incidentally those who have watched the African dervishes whirl madly in the jungle clearings have no difficulty in tracing the origin of the primitive emotionalism expressed in the "Shakerism" of the 18th century.

Following the course of history, we find that later, Greece also turned to Egypt as a source of knowledge. Among others, the great mathematician and philosopher of the sixth century B. C.— Pythagoras, the Greek apostle of Reincarnation, whose name is familiar through his Table even in elementary schools, was initiated in Egyptian temples.

Due to the influence of teachings received there, Pythagoras believed in the Soul as "a thought of God." To him, our future lives are contingent upon what part of the present existence we give to selfish pursuits, to the world, and to God. He regarded the body simply as one of a succession of "receptacles" for the housing of the Soul. He taught that mathematical relations underlie all things according to the Law of Numbers. He taught also that in Reincarnation was embodied the Law of Universal and Immutable Justice, and that in its truth lay the explanation of the apparent inequalities of life. Incidentally, he agreed with the oldest Egyptian teachers, that the highest element is Fire, expressing divinity in nature.

The moral and spiritual value given to numbers by this "Sage of Samos" as he is sometimes called, can be traced directly to Egyptian records of at least twelve centuries before him. The brotherhood of Pythagoreans which he founded, followed also the Egyptian rather than the Chaldean or Hindu concepts, and, as in Egypt, initiation in this order meant the unfolding of all available knowledge, which was not the case in the Asiatic organizations.

It can be said of Pythagoras, whom some of the early Fathers of the Church sought to identify with Gautama Siddhartha—Buddha—that he laid the scientific basis of the doctrine of Reincarnation, **as Christ later laid its spiritual foundation.**

After Pythagoras, another great Greek philosopher, Plato, pupil of Socrates, and author of the great books, "Timaeus," "Republic," and "Laws," also taught the principle of re-birth. He invariably expressed great admiration for the Pythagorean teachings and for mathematics. He was also initiated in Egyptian temples and his philosophical view of the universe is in accordance with the teachings of Egyptian priests. The similarity of his teachings and the inner meaning of Mosaic writings, was recognized by those who lived in the early days of Christianity, to the extent that he was called "a Moses with an Attic tongue," and conversely, Moses was called "the Jewish Plato."

It can readily be seen that so far, Science and Reincarnation were closely allied. Furthermore, we find that the great religious books of antiquity, the Bible, Kaballah, Zohar, Tao-Teh King, The Book of the Dead, and others, also conveyed the great principle of re-birth. Thus, there are in the Bible many quotations that can only be construed in the light of this belief, while in the Kaballah and Zohar we are told of the repeated embodiments experienced by the Soul.

The sacred books of the Magi, who unerringly found the birthplace of Christ from Chaldea, tell us that purification of Soul is attained by means of many reincarnations. That the Magi were a very scientific body is evidenced by the fact that there is official record of their astronomical activities in the Valley of the Euphrates as early as the eighth century B. C. The Wise Men of the East, or Magi, who sought out the infant Jesus, bearing Him costly gifts, would hardly have been interested in His coming, if His teachings, the trend of which was prophesied long before His birth, were to be in conflict with their basic belief.

Following Plato, there arose in Greece the Sceptics—agnostics of our day—closely allied to the doctrines known as Epicurean and Stoic. Drifting away from the great truth of Re-birth, they also became enemies of true Science, represented by mathematics, and went so far as to deny all Science through Empiricus, one of their leading authors, in the fourth to third century B. C. By thus accepting the dogma of Ignorance—as did the Roman Church through the Middle Ages— their darkened minds rejected all scientific truth, including the theory of Aristarchus, a Pythagorean, who in 250 B. C. tried to prove that the earth revolved around the sun. His knowledge was declared to be "impious" and strangely enough, when the Italian Galileo brought this truth again to light almost two thousand years later, he was also declared to be "impious" by the Tribunal of the Inquisition.

Notwithstanding the attacks of the Sceptics, the teachings of Pythagoras and Plato were carried on in Syracuse, Sicily, by Archimedes who demonstrated the same wonderful knowledge that Pythagoras had expressed, not only in mathematics, but also in astronomy and in physics. Through his discovery of the endless screw and his famous lever theory: that given the proper lever the earth could be lifted, and through other fundamental scientific truths, his name is as familiar to the student as that of the Sage of Samos. His efforts saved Science, threatened by the Sceptics, and his work remains as another powerful link in the great chain of progress forged by the Egyptian mathematicians, and by his great predecessors, Pythagoras and Plato—the chain in which are invariably linked together scientific truth and spiritual insight.

More than once in the darkest periods of history, when Science was at a stand-still, and ignorance and doubt held sway, the beacon light that can never be extinguished—**Reincarnation**—pointed the way through the gloom and depression to greater attainment and progress.

After Archimedes, the ignorant Stoics gained

control of the rulers of the Roman Empire which had superseded Greece in power, and the world was blindly groping in this dark crisis of spiritual night, when there dawned on the horizon "the bright and morning Star," "the Light of the World"— Christ, the Reincarnationist.

CHAPTER II

CHRIST THE REINCARNATIONIST

During the period when the Jews had fallen under the yoke of the Roman Empire, after bending under that of the Egyptians, Assyrians, and Babylonians, the greatest of all Reincarnationists came: the Nazarene. His early life was such as to imbue Him with deep understanding and compassion for struggling humanity. He was born in a stable; His youth and young manhood were spent in the humble environment of a carpenter's home in Nazareth with no advantages of wealth or education.

Yet from the first He was a child prodigy. We are told in the Scriptures that at the age of twelve He astonished the learned doctors of the Temple in Jerusalem by His answers to their questions. "They found Him in the Temple sitting in the midst of the doctors, both hearing them and asking them questions." When his parents chided Him for his truancy from their side, He replied in dawning comprehension of His divine mission: "Wist ye not that I must be about my Father's business?"

CHRISTIANITY CRUCIFIED

Although historical information is meagre concerning His early manhood, there is no doubt that later, in preparation for His great ministry, Jesus was initiated—like John the Baptist—by Essenian priests who dwelt in the Jordan wilderness. Also in Egypt—the latter fact being evidenced by one of the main accusations of the Jews against Him: that he was a sorcerer who had learned magic in the Egyptian temples.

Such knowledge as was disseminated to initiates was however of a very different nature. It was that which had been imparted almost six centuries before to Pythagoras—the probable master of Buddha—giving Him mastery not only in mathematics, but in music, astronomy, and medicine, and in a word, the whole range of "physics" the Greek expression of Universal Knowledge. That knowledge has been described at length by some of the foremost scientists of the day, such as Thouvenin of the Academy of Sciences in Paris; the deeper enlightenment that even now puzzles Science and which inspired, long before the name of Israel was historically recorded, such wonderful works as the Tomb of King Khufu, known as the First Pyramid of Gizeh, where "optical" joints of one ten-thousandth of an inch unite gigantic blocks over acres of space.

Together with this unparalleled scientific knowledge, leading to control over all the elements, the belief in Reincarnation was taken for granted by Christ as by those to whom He was now to preach. To teach the principle of re-birth was indeed superfluous. Deep-rooted in the oldest Greek, Assyrian, and Egyptian spiritual thought, it was also an integral part of Judaism itself. Thus we see in the Jewish book of Zohar that the individual life is only a "link" in a great chain of existences.

This great belief was really the fundamental key-note of the "Mysteries" that Christ came to give to the world. The scene was laid for His coming, as expressed in the words of St. Augustine, one of the early Fathers of the Christian Church, known to all theologians: "What is now called the Christian religion **already existed among the ancients,** and was not lacking at the very beginnings of the human race. When Christ appeared in the flesh, the true religion already in existence received the name of Christian."

It should be clearly understood that the Nazarene did not come to teach a new doctrine. He came to spread abroad in terms intelligible to the masses, the truths that were already known to those conversant with the inner teachings of the oldest spiritual beliefs; He appeared as a concrete living example of the attainment possible to all who followed such truths.

To those who lacked sufficient enlightenment to grasp the full significance of His words, He elucidated by means of parables—akin to mythology. He sought to awaken His followers to the consciousness of their innate divinity as the stepping-stone to further advancement: "My Father and your Father, my God and your God." When they marvelled at His miracles, He gave them the divine assurance: "These things shall ye do **and more also.**" Pointing the way to a deeper comprehension of the spiritual life, He said, "Neither shall ye say 'Lo here! or Lo there! for the kingdom of heaven is **within you.**'"

And opening up before them the gateway to illimitable attainment, He gave the inspiring command: "Be ye therefore **perfect,** even as your Father which is in heaven is perfect."

One proof of the fact that Reincarnation was taken then as a matter of course, is shown by the question of Jesus to His disciples: "Whom do men say that I, **the son of Man,** am?" And they answered, "Some say that thou art John the Baptist, some Elias (Elijah), and others Jeremias, or one of the prophets."

The form of the question indicates that Christ meant only His physical self—"the son of Man." He came to bring the Word—true enlightenment from God—and would have rebuked the disciples if their answer had revealed mere superstition; indeed He would not have elicited such an answer.

He continued by His next question to point out the greater truth concerning the true Ego—the **I**. "But whom say ye that **I** am?" And Simon Peter answered and said, "Thou art the Christ, the son of the living God." It was because of the advancement and spiritual vision of Peter, who looked beyond the physical to the divine, that Christ then and there pronounced the words: "Thou art Peter (a rock) and upon this rock (the rock of spiritual vision)—will I build my Church."

Another convincing proof that even the most skeptical cannot refute, that Christ was a believer in Reincarnation, is contained in all four gospels—in conflict on so many important points, and yet all agreeing that Christ in His own words declared

John the Baptist to be the reincarnation of Elijah, the prophet of the Old Testament.*

In another instance Christ told His disciples, "I go to prepare a place for you. And if I go and prepare a place for you, I will come again and receive you unto Myself, that where I am, there ye may be also." Again, referring to His second coming, He said, **"This generation** shall not pass away until all these things shall come to pass."

Christ herein stated that at the time of His second coming, or voluntary reincarnation, the very persons to whom He addressed those words would be present on the earth. His words can be construed logically in no other way, and the facts stated could not be accomplished except through the reincarnation of "this generation." That His second coming was to be another reincarnation in the flesh is evidenced by His words at the Last Supper: "I will not drink of the fruit of the vine, until the kingdom of God shall come." **"A spirit hath not flesh and bones"** and cannot drink wine.

Jesus invariably taught the immutable working of Justice: "As a man soweth that shall he also reap." He pointed out that rewards and punish-

---

* See "Biblical Proofs of Reincarnation," by the same authors.

ments are to be meted out on the same plane in which the deeds that merited them are committed, as indicated by His words to one of His followers who would have defended Him against the Jews come to take Him: "Put up thy sword again into its place, **for all they that take the sword shall perish with the sword."**

The "Beatitudes," and the "Woes" that follow in St. Luke's version, teach that all must pass through every phase of human experience. The law of Justice plays no favorites. The wealthy idler of today will be the beggar of the future existence; the industrious, humble worker may be the great leader in another life; the happy and care-free will taste of misery. To attain perfection of understanding, every form of earthly relationship must be experienced, every shade of affection and desire, every variety of conflict and temptation. The Soul must experience all the joys and sorrows of all forms of life, to insure its full development. How can this possibly be achieved in one short life time?

The Nazarene was indeed "the Light of the World" come to reveal the true God to man, a God of infinite Justice, whom He was continually exhorting the people to follow. His delineation of the Father in no way remotely resembles the tribal God of the Jews depicted in the Old Testament.

Consider these words of Jehovah: "And when the Lord thy God hath delivered it (the city) into thy hand, thou shalt smite every male thereof with the the edge of the sword; but the women and the little ones, and the cattle and all that is in the city, even the spoil thereof thou shalt take unto thyself . . . But of the cities of those people which the Lord thy God shall give thee for an inheritance, thou shalt save alive nothing that breatheth, but thou shalt destroy them utterly." (Deut. 20:13, 14, 16) . . . **"And thou shalt eat of the fruit of thine own body, the flesh of thy sons and thy daughters,** which the Lord thy God hath given thee, in the siege and straitness wherewith thine enemies shall distress thee." (Deut. 28:53.)

Like a healing benediction, in startling contrast, come the gentle words of Christ: "But love ye your enemies, and do good, and lend hoping for nothing again; and your reward shall be great, and ye shall be the children of the Highest, **for He is kind unto the unthankful and to the evil."** (St. Luke 6:35.)

The terrible Jehovah thundered forth his vindictive commands to destroy, to despoil innocent women and children. Christ taught: "For with what measure ye mete it shall be measured to you again." If those who obeyed the dictates of Jehovah indeed received measure for measure, what harvest of horrors they would reap in future incarnations!

The prophet Micah, contemporary of Isaiah, prophesied of the coming of Christ: "But thou, Bethlehem, though thou be least among the thousand of Judah, yet out of thee shall he come forth unto me that is to be ruler in Israel, **whose goings out have been from of old, from everlasting.**"

And Christ, the son of Man and Son of God, He who has attained perfection of divinity and union with God after countless "goings out" or reincarnations, looks down on struggling humanity today, sees the pitiful efforts of the "blind leading the blind," hears the constant blasphemy against His Father, the gross misinterpretation of His holy Word fostered from the beginning of the Christian Church through the ignorance, intolerance, and bigotry of those who called themselves His ministers, and crucified again in spirit on the Cross He cries in pitying tenderness, "Father, forgive them, for they know not what they do!"

CHAPTER III

EARLY CHRISTIANITY

The divine Word had come to earth through Christ, and it was the tremendous task of His followers to "make disciples of all the nations," to preach the Gospel "unto the uttermost parts of the earth."

Christ had left no word in writing. Why? This mystery has never been made clear; it may be of interest and significance to consider in this connection, that initiation in the Temples of ancient knowledge involved certain rules not to be disobeyed.

Except for the record of the New Testament, there is little coherent history of the early Church during the Apostolic Age. Paul, whose Hebrew name was Saul, a Roman Jew, is the most outstanding of the apostles—all of them Jews. There is no evidence that he knew anything of Christ's ministry except by report. In his interpretation of the teachings of Jesus, there are traces of his early rabbinic learning under the Elder Gamaliel, together with elements of Platonism. As a theologian he is often at variance with the concept of Christ as presented by the Gospels. His interpretation differed radically from that of Mark which followed later.

Truly the founding of Christian theology was a complicated task! From the very outset there was conflict in the Church due to Paul's belligerent attitude on certain points. The great difficulty was concerning the question of rites, such as circumcision, to which Christ Himself had submitted. These rites were still enforced by Peter and the other apostles, who claimed them to be an integral part of the new religion, as they were in the old synagogue.

According to Peter and John, heathens could not become Christians without first submitting to these rites. Heathens had in other words, to become Jews before being admitted to the Christian Church. Paul resolutely discarded and refuted this belief, thus renouncing completely his own Jewish origin, and asserting himself not as a Roman-Jew but simply as a Roman.

This attitude of Paul brought about an acute conflict between him and Peter. The latter was now the head of the first Christian community in the world, that in Jerusalem. The Jews could not very well admit this new organization founded on the teachings of a man sentenced by them as an imposter. Persecutions were started, and in the year 37 A. D. the first victim, St. Stephen, was stoned to death.

The dissension between Peter and Paul became more pronounced, Paul going so far as to accuse Peter of living like a heathen. In 50 A. D. Paul was made to appear before a meeting of the Apostles in the city of Antioch, and explain his activities. It was decided that Paul would preach to the heathen and Peter to the Jews. The difficulty did not stop there, however. Great objection was raised against Peter by the Christian-Jews for accepting a seat at the same table with non-circumcised converted heathen. Peter had to yield lest he lose the converted Jews, and even Barnabas, the great friend of Paul, took sides with Peter. For a time it looked as if a deadlock would ensue, and the chasm between Christian-Jews and the other Christians could not be bridged.

Finally the greater will power of Paul won out. However, Peter left Palestine for Rome, where both he and Paul preached. In 64 A. D. Emperor Nero found a new distraction in the burning of Rome. This led to additional persecutions against the Christians, falsely accused of starting the conflagration, and both Peter and Paul died then, the first on the Cross, but head down, and the second under the sword—thanks to his citizenship that saved him from a more infamous death.

Nowhere had Christ said that Rome should be chosen as the center of the new religion. Emperor Titus had destroyed Jerusalem, and Christianity was to gain its greatest momentum in the Roman capital. As early as the beginning of the second century, monarchial bishopric came into being under Ignatius, Bishop of Antioch. There is no record of how this position of authority arose. Clement of Rome, writing before the time of Ignatius, traced back the existence of church officers to "apostolic succession." His view is historically inaccurate, based on a misconception of Paul's statement. (Cor. 16:15, 16.) Ignatius himself knew nothing of apostolic succession, yet before the middle of the second century, the power of the bishopric was immeasurably enhanced thereby.

At first Clement as bishop of Rome, had no more power than the bishop of Corinth, as proven by his correspondence in about 94 A. D. Gradually, however, St. Clement, helped greatly by Ignatius, succeeded in giving to himself a sort of central power, which was to become two centuries later, organized papacy, or unity of the Roman church.

The Church was already falling into the error of seeking temporal power and authority, due to the acceptance of the Jehovah of the Old Testament instead of the God of Christ. Ignatius was an enemy of all free thinking; he said "Shun divergences as the beginning of evils. **Follow your bishop** as Christ followed His Father."

The Gnostics who came into power during this period sought to change the false conceptions of the Church. Believers in Reincarnation, they could not accept the theory of "original sin" and a wrathful God appeased by the sacrifice of His only Son. They were bitterly opposed by the Roman Church, but they increased in numbers and power, many of the more intellectual members adopting their views.

The seeds of intolerance that later fructified into hatred and bloodshed, were already being sown. The Roman Church claimed that it alone had the power, through apostolic succession, to interpret the teachings of Christ. The divergences in apostolic preaching were reconciled according to the private opinions of the leaders of the Church.

It was during this period that Marcion, the first Church reformer, a believer in Reincarnation, tried to purge the Church of its adherence to the Yahweh of the Jews. He was to become the head of the Marcionites, whose influence later extended over Egypt, Italy, Syria, Persia, Arabia, and other countries. He taught that the war-like and cruel Deity must be rejected by all true Christians, as utterly inconsistent with the delineation of God the Father, by Christ. As a result of his teachings he was excommunicated, and founded his own church in 144 A. D., compiling for its use, the first canon, including the Epistles of Paul and the Gospel of St. Luke: the first authoritative collection of New Testament writings. His churches lasted until the fifth century. There is no record of his own later history.

As a result of the internal dissension, the Roman Church tightened the reins of authority; definite creeds were formulated, rigid doctrines were adopted, and at the close of the second century the "Catholic Church" had developed its distinguishing characteristics. (The word "Catholic" had first been used by Ignatius, as meaning "universal.") The power of the bishops was strengthened, a collection of authoritative New Testament writings recognized; and the Church became a strong corporate body with official leaders. Hereafter only those were recognized as Christians who acknowledged the Creed, the New Testament Canon, and the authority of the bishops.

All disputes that arose were settled arbitrarily; the Roman Church claiming the right to formulate all the creeds and sacraments and the details of observance. For example: dissension had arisen between the churches of Asia Minor and Syria, and the Roman Church, over the observance of Easter. Asia Minor observed it by the Lord's Supper on the eve of the fourteenth of the month Nisan, as was the oldest custom. The Romans observed it on the Sabbath, regardless of the date. The problem was complicated by the fact that the Gospels disagreed on the date: John holding that Christ died on the fourteenth Nisan, and the other Gospels that His death occurred on the fifteenth. The churches of Asia Minor refused to conform to the observance of the Roman Church and were excommunicated. Rome had become the greatest and most influential center of Christianity, and was drifting away from the true spirit of the teachings of Christ.

In these days, the great School of Alexandria, founded by Alexander the Great in 332 B. C., was the center of culture and learning; the meeting ground of Greek philosophy, Judaism, Oriental cults, and all the older Egyptian and other teachings. It was the leading cosmopolitan city of the world; its library was the most famous and extensive in the empire. There the Old Testament was translated into Greek, and there Philo reinterpreted Judaism into terms of Greek philosophy.

Nothing is known of the introduction of Christianity in this center, but it must have been early, since the first historical records show it firmly rooted. The Gnostic and Reincarnationist, Basilides, had taught there in the beginning of the second century. In the early part of the third century, the great Origen, a Reincarnationist, and true founder of Christian theology, became the Head of the School, and produced his marvellous writings. He was ordained a presbyter by the Palestinian bishops to give him freedom to preach. This aroused the jealousy of the bishop of Alexandria, Demetrius, and as a result, Origen was banished from Alexandria. He continued his writings and studies in Caesarea. In the great Decian persecution that followed, he was imprisoned and tortured, and died as a result of this cruel treatment— **a martyr for the cause of true Christianity!**

The theological structure founded by Origen is

the most remarkable achievement of any Christian scholar. He was a man of lofty principles, of great purity of character, and lived a blameless life. His monumental work, "Hexapala," giving the Hebrew and four parallel Greek translations of the Old Testament, and a long series of commentaries on the whole range of Scripture, is the most valuable work given to the Christian world. His writings were of enormous scope; he stands out as a true pillar of the Church, and exponent of the Word. Had the Church continued to build on the true scientific theology founded by him, its succeeding history might have been entirely different. But the true conception of Christ was clouded by the haunting picture of the jealous and angry deity of old Jewish tradition.

Then came St. Augustine, born in 354 A. D., at first a Manichaean—Reincarnationist—but later the most orthodox of Christians. His teachings were in flagrant contradiction of all the laws of Justice. All men are born in sin—"sinners in Adams"; but their sinful state is rendered much worse by the manner of their conception—the deadly sin of "concupiscence." The whole human race is "a mass of perdition," even to the youngest infant, and as such deserves the wrath of God. No man can attain salvation without partaking of the sacraments of the Church; infants who die before sacrament can be administered are condemned to everlasting punishment. It mattered not that Christ had said: "Suffer little children to come unto me, for of such is the kingdom of heaven."

Augustine stressed the authority of the Scriptures as interpreted by the Roman Church, and admitted no other guidance. Yet he said, "I should not believe in the truth of the Gospels, unless the **authority** of the Catholic Church **forced** me to do so" (cf. p. 143) He maintained that nothing was to be believed save on this authority; he believed in the **infallibility** of the **interpretation,** rather than the infallibility of the Scriptures themselves—as do many Christians to this day. Yet this same interpretation has forged the shackles of fear and the burden of "original sin" on the masses, and has brought about their servile subjection to the tyranny of Church leaders who claim that they alone can outline the way of salvation.

The viewpoint of St. Augustine was undoubtedly colored by his own deep remorse and sense of sin, and soured with the sensual surfeit of his early life, as depicted in his "Confessions." How different is the teaching of the pure-minded Origen, the

Reincarnationist! He said, "We do not sin because of the first man having sinned, but the first man sinned for the same reason that we do: because he was still a child in spiritual evolution, and we ourselves are far from having reached perfection."

Yet Augustine, a self-confessed former dissolute, was created a saint, and Origen, whose life was infinitely more Christ-like in every sense, was left without anything approaching due recognition by the Church. Papacy thrived on the subjugation and fear of the people; how could Justice be expected of those who worshipped an unjust and cruel Deity?

Somehow, one is compelled to think that after all, deep in his innermost being, Augustine was always the Platonist and Manichaean, who wrote in his "Confessions" "Did I not live in another body before entering my mother's womb?"

Many of the early Fathers and leaders of the Church agreed with the belief and teachings of Reincarnation: Basilides, 140 A. D., head of the Basilideans; Tatian the Apologist; Valentinius, the most scientific of all the Gnostics; Plotinus, who wrote fifty-seven treatises after the age of fifty; Porphyry, his disciple; Manes, head of the Manichaeans; St. Jerome; St. Pamphilius; St. Gregory; Jamblichus, a great mathematician and believer in the Law of Numbers, who wrote "The Return of the Soul"; and Arthenagoras—to cite these only of a long, formidable list.

The philosopher, Philo, the only contemporary of Christ whose writings have been preserved, was another great Reincarnationist. He knew, as taught by the Nazarene, that there is no way for any religion to explain that God does not create Evil, except through the truth of Reincarnation. The power of "free will" that we inherit as living Souls, at each re-birth, constitutes us arbiters of our successive destinies. Evil is created by our failure to act in accordance with the higher guidance, through clinging to the sensual pleasures of the earthly plane. If we shut our eyes to the light we naturally stumble and fall. If a child stumbles and falls when learning to walk, is it because of evil created by the parent? Reincarnation teaches that we only reap the evil that we sow; this is in strict accordance with the re-iterated words of Christ.

It is not to be wondered at that during this same fourth century, St. Jerome was able to maintain publicly in a debate with Vigilantius, that **the ma-**

jority of Christians of his day were Reincarnationists! St. Jerome was a prominent figure in the Church; he translated the whole Bible into Latin, proving his scholarship by going back beyond the Septuagint to the original Hebrew, and incurred the displeasure of St. Augustine by producing in too simple terms "The Vulgate," which is the only version still recognized by the Catholic Church.

Like the Nazarene, Jerome believed in simplicity of life, habits, and worship: ". . . pray not to be heard of men." But those who accepted the false doctrines of the Church were rapidly drifting away from the original teachings of Jesus. Pomp and glory were the order of the day, rather than the simplicity of the One who said, "My kingdom is not of this world." Ornaments of Assyrian and Babylonian origin were now being worn; proud heads that professed to follow the One crowned with thorns were richly adorned with mitres set with blazing jewels. In defiance of the true humility of Christ, the temporal power of the Church was being organized with swords to back it. The temptations of the lower forces were not resisted; "the kingdoms of the world and the glory of them" were too alluring.

To attain and maintain supreme power and authority, the people must not have any other leaders who might teach them equality and justice. So was born the Decree of Anathema against all Reincarnationists, obtained from the eastern Emperor Justinian, by the Church and Council of Constantinople in 553 A. D. A post-mortem was held over the long dead martyred Origen; he was declared a "heretic," by a small majority after lengthy debates, and thus by the basest act of gross injustice and ingratitude ever recorded in the annals of history, **Reincarnation and the true teachings of Christ were outlawed from the Roman Church.**

CHAPTER IV

CRUCIFIXION

Like a dark and deep canyon between lofty mountains, the promulgation of the Justinian Decree in the middle of the sixth century, marks the definite dividing line between true and false Christianity— true Christianity as taught by Christ, its cornerstone now blasphemed as "heresy," and the false Christianity established by the Roman Church.

The Justinian Decree was destroying hope for the world through its repudiation of the belief in re-birth. It was creating a changeling Justice—a Justice for sale to those who would pay the price. The true motive of the Church was the accumulation of riches and the gaining of additional temporal power. With characteristic cleverness and diplomacy, advantage was taken of existing circumstances: of the rivalry between Rome in the west, bending before Gothic invasions, and Constantinople in the east, where the Roman influence survived.

In the eastern capital, bishops were ordered to gather who could be used as tools for the denunciation of the Reincarnation belief. The Church also relied on the easily flattered Emperor Justinian to carry out the execution of the decree under his name in a most efficient and destructive manner. Forgotten were the words of Christ rebuking Peter for using his weapon in legitimate defence of his Master. "By sword and fire" became indeed the new motto of the Roman Church.

The enforcement of anathema against Reincarnationists commenced on a vast scale, and there followed an era of persecution against them without parallel in history. Available records show that in the period from the days of Justinian to the tenth century, more than two hundred thousand Manichaeans—Reincarnationists—were put to death on account of their belief.

A salient episode of this great persecution—the rule of Fear—is shown in the murder in 590 A. D. of Emperor Maurice, in the same city of Constantinople, where the Justinian Decree had been issued. History tells us that he was put to death after seeing his sons tortured and beheaded, while the Empress, who had relied on the sacredness of the walls of "Santa Sophia" as a refuge, was seized there, together with her three daughters. Torture and death followed for them in a most barbarous manner; friends and adherents in large numbers were included in the massacre.

That centurion Phocas carried out this fearful plot at the instigation of the then Pope Gregory and his advisors, is evidenced by the exultation shown by the Church ruler on receiving the news, and his public congratulations and prayers for Phocas!

When we delve into the obscure reason for such an inhuman and anti-Christian attitude on the part of the Head of the Church, we find that Maurice was a Marcionite—Reincarnationist—and an initiated Magi! The proof of this is given historically. One of the secret rules of the Magi was mutual assistance and defence. Maurice had a warm friend and admirer in King Chosroes of Persia, also a Reincarnationist and Magi, whom he had helped attain the throne. Upon hearing of his assassination, Chosroes declared war—not in revenge, but in Justice—stormed Jerusalem, burned the Sepulchre, and the Churches as now ruled by "murderers and liars," and finally sent the Holy Cross to Persia.

A momentous event indeed! Some six hundred years before, other Magi, Kings, and Reincarnationists, had stopped in that same city on their way to the humble birthplace of Christ in nearby Bethlehem. Now Chosroes, also Magi, King, and Reincarnationist, was given the power to remove the symbol of His sacrifice supreme—the holy Cross —from the very place where it had been erected. **The answer of God to the defiance of Rome: Reincarnation, the Truth!**

The Church and the world gasped in astonishment! Yet the brutal fact remained: the Cross had been carried away, and the proud Romans had to pay tribute. The true "abomination of the desolation" foretold by the prophets had come. There is no doubt that the head of the Church and his chieftains cringed, and for a moment turned their haggard faces to the light. But having once tasted of power they could not resist the pressure of wordly temptations. They began to plot anew for vengeance and for further conquests.

Notwithstanding their terrible losses, the Manichaeans had not been entirely destroyed, on the contrary many of their branches flourished in various centers. One of them particularly, the Albigenses, obtained considerable influence in southern France. It reached the height of its power in about 1020, and created great uneasiness in Rome. Finally, after a synod called for that purpose, a crusade of extermination against the Albigenses—Reincarnationists—was ordered by Pope Innocent III. His Christian (!) feelings are well expressed by his historical command at that time: **"Kill them all—God will recognize His own!"**

There followed an almost absolute execution of his order, and rivers of blood again ran freely. A Pope was now riding a war-horse, brandishing a sword in defiance of the teachings of Christ, yet ostensibly in the name of the Cross!

During the first part of this persecution of the Albigenses, there was born in 1033, the second St. Augustine, the student and thinker, St. Anselm. He discovered in his search for knowledge that scientific thought was confined almost entirely to the Arabian philosophers, who had become prominent through the Mohammedan conquest, and who were represented by such thinkers as Avicenna of Ispahan, and later by Averroes. These Reincarnationists were akin to the Pythagoreans, and so carried on the mathematical principles related both to life and science, their numerological expressions being in use to this day.

St. Anselm, always ardent defender of the infallibility of the Roman Church, nevertheless absorbed so much of the Oriental philosophy as to express himself often as a disciple of Plato: for instance, in his theory of "Eternal Ideas." He saw God as the "unitary Being"—a conception that would lead naturally to the teachings of Pythagoras.

Fortified by the Anselmian theory of infallibility, the Roman Church rose to great heights of temporal power during that period. The papal banner floated over England through the conquest of William the Conqueror. In reward, men from Normandy were made bishops at Canterbury and other important points in Great Britain, thus insuring spiritual as well as physical control over the land.

During the same century that banner floated also over all that had been the German Empire. It had reigned supreme over France and later over Spain since the memorable year 732, when Charles Martel checked the Mohammedan flood of conquest rushing in from Africa, on the battlefield of Poitiers.

Two hundred years later, St. Thomas Aquinas, pupil of the Mystic Albertus Magnus, perforce borrowed from the same Arabic sources of knowledge as St. Anselm, and confronted with the Pythagorean thought, sought to evade the issue by borrowing also from the Jewish philosopher Maimonides. He thus created the Aristotlean-Catholic system of philosophy, which was supposed, among other things, to disprove scientifically both the teachings of Pythagoras and Reincarnation. But, as we shall see later, Science was to rise again and crush the weak Aristotlean foundation, and the light of Reincarnation was to blaze forth again within the very walls of the Vatican.

The Truth could not be obliterated. With the Albigenses almost exterminated in France, other Reincarnationists had continued to carry the belief elsewhere. In the 14th century ,John Huss, a Bohemian disciple of John Wycliffe—known by his first translation of the whole Bible into English in 1382—organized a religious movement admitting re-birth into the concept of Christianity. The influence of the Hussites spread greatly over Germany and Holland, and through affiliations, in Great Britain. After the Council of Constance had condemned both his religious theories and those of Wycliffe, John Huss was burned alive at the stake as a heretic in 1415.

During the 15th century, there arose a Reincarnationist in the very midst of the Church, a man of great scientific knowledge and a trained mathematician. He was Cardinal Nicholas de Cusa, of the diocese of Treves, who first wrote in one of his books, "De Docta Ignorantis"—"To my mind the earth turns upon its axis in a day and a night." Like Pythagoras and Philo, he attributed a spiritual value to numbers, and there was no doubt in his mind about the plurality of existences and of the fact that other planets are inhabited. He maintained this belief in the Vatican itself in such a forcible and convincing manner as to gain the approval and encouragement of both Popes Eugene IV and Nicholas V.

Again it is significant that Science and Reincarnation were rising together. Following the constructive work of Cardinal de Cusa, like the first glimpse of blue in a sky darkened with heavy clouds, a new philosophy was created in Italy during the same century, by two eminent scholars: Ficinus and Pico de Mirandola, the father of modern occultism. Basically that philosophy was a revival of Neoplatonism—which at all times spells Reincarnation—and an attempt on the part of Ficinus to unite it with Christianity.

Mirandola had discovered added evidence of the great belief in re-birth left us by Christ, in other sacred books of the Orient, particularly the Jewish Kaballah, which he put on a par with the Bible.

The movement extended to Germany, where it met with considerable success.

Meanwhile the Roman Church was fast sinking into an abyss of iniquity. Pope Alexander VI appeared on the scene, who through his four adulterine children, led the infamous dynasty of the Borgias, in which Lucrezia Borgia won the most horrible renown of any woman in history, most of her crimes being planned within the Vatican. Her brother, Caesar Borgia, one of the most sinister figures in history, guided by Machiavelli, known as "the great Deceiver," ruled over both the Vatican and his family as a despot. Discarding his religious vestments and vows alike, he married a French princess, and proceeded to write the bloodiest page of papal history. Poison became the popular means of extermination, especially where wealthy cardinals must be suppressed. This proved Borgia's undoing. At a supper where Cardinal Castellesi was to be removed through this subtle agency, a mistake on the part of a servant caused the fatal poison to be distributed to all present. Pope Alexander VI died from the effects; Caesar barely escaped and never completely recovered, dying in obscurity a few years later in Spain.

Nearing the days of Pope Leo X, in the early

sixteenth century, the Church had gone completely astray from the true teachings of Christ. It had become a new Temple where everything, from "indulgences" to consciences, was for sale; conditions reminiscent of the days when Christ made His denunciation, **"My Father's house is a house of prayer, but ye have made it a den of thieves!"** All conscientious historians are agreed that these were indeed days of almost pure paganism for Rome, with Greek gods replacing Christian images. Christianity was indeed being crucified by those who should have extolled it. Dark clouds were fast gathering from all sides over the sin center of the Vatican.

"And there was darkness over all the earth," until at length, "the veil of the Temple was rent in twain," and amid the thunder and lightning of the storms of denunciation of truth-seekers, Protestantism was born, and hope resurrected anew for the world.

CHAPTER V

RESURRECTION

It was in 1510 that Martin Luther, then an Augustinian monk, went to Rome and witnessed there the orgies taking place in the very midst of the Roman Church. What he saw and heard was enough to raise doubt in his mind. "Why does the Pope, who is richer than Croesus, build up 'St. Peter' with his own funds, instead of using the money of the poor?" he asked.

His pertinent questions and criticisms were enough to start like a trail of burning powder, the movement known since as Protestantism. It spread as if by magic through Germany. Had not the blasphemous Pope Leo X gone so far as to say **"The fairy tale of Christ** has helped us and our own also!"

The hand of Justice that had led Chosroes to Jerusalem, led now the armies of Charles V in whose ranks were many Lutherans, against Rome, and in 1527 the imperial troops took the city and devastated the surrounding towns, making Pope and cardinals prisoners. A mock synod was gathered, and Luther was made "Pope," while cardinals were paraded on donkeys in the streets by the German lansquenets (soldiers).

This insult shook the Roman Church to its very foundations. Yet, rooted in evil, it would not repent. With renewed assistance from the same satanic forces that had tempted Christ, it rapidly succeeded in re-acquiring great temporal power, still adhering to its policy of persecution.

Some time before, in 1492, the new continent of America had been discovered by Columbus, in contravention of the belief of the learned men of the Roman Church. Both their theology and science were now to be threatened by more direct attacks. In 1532 John Calvin of France, claiming divine inspiration, had suddenly and publicly sided with both the sarcastic Erasmus of Rotterdam and with Luther of Germany. Under his youthful leadership, French Protestantism became well organized, after he had dared to defend his cause in a public letter to Francis I, then Catholic ruler in France. After persecution, he established his stronghold in Switzerland, and created in Calvinism what was no more than an offspring of Lutherism, with an extremely mediaeval and narrow conception as to the relation of Church and State.

However, thanks to his erudition, Calvin's own

influence extended beyond Switzerland and France to England, Scotland, Germany, and the Netherlands. His work added to that of Luther, weakened the spiritual power of the Roman Church, and to a greater extent its temporal authority. But, like Luther, Calvin failed to realize that the fundamental principle of Christianity, deliberately discarded by the Roman Church, was vitally necessary to establish unity and justice in the Protestant Church, and that without the great truth of Reincarnation it was merely **"a house divided against itself."**

The Roman Church retaliated by all means in its power against the attacks of Protestantism. The devastation of Rome by the Germans had left a burning scar that could not be healed; the Church had no concept of the divine forgiveness of Christ.

The Reformist party had grown strong in France, and invaded the higher circles of society and intellectual thought. It was decided to strike a decisive blow there. The regent of France, Catherine de Medici, was a niece of Pope Gregory XIII and both showed great ingenuity in formulating plots. It was easy to reach an understanding. During the historical night of St. Bartholomew, August 24, 1572, the fatal words heard against the Albigenses,

"Kill them all!" were repeated, and a massacre was started in Paris that extended to the other parts of France and numbered among its many victims, leading Calvinists, such as Admiral Coligny.

As in the days when Emperor Maurice had been assassinated, there was great rejoicing in Rome. The Pope himself sang a special "Te Deum" and various commemorations were ordered to record this crushing blow to the Protestant enemy. Thus encouraged, Gregory began to help in every possible way the Irish revolt against Queen Elizabeth of England, stopping short of no means to further his plans.

Still Protestantism progressed. In Sweden, King Wasa forced his people to accept Lutherism as the official religion, already recognized as such by other great nations led by England. Even in France, threatened by powerful enemies, the diplomatic Henry IV issued the Edict of Nantes, which gave an apparent religious freedom to the survivors of the St. Bartholomew butchery. This action did not particularly please Rome, more interested in its own temporal gain than in the political situation of France, and the fanatic monk Ravaillac rewarded Henry IV, one of the noblest French kings, by stabbing him to death.

CHRISTIANITY CRUCIFIED

In 1534 Ignatius of Loyola had founded the famous order of Jesuits, the subsequent right arm of the Roman Church. A little later, the Index system was created, another weapon, by means of which all writings, the world over, were to be censored, and all those conflicting or disagreeing with the Roman dogma, expressly forbidden and condemned.

Subsequently, the Papacy succeeded in establishing in succession, Cardinals Mazarin and Richelieu as real directors of French affairs of state. This led in 1685 to the revocation of the Edict of Nantes, thereby making Protestantism illegal in France under the severest penalties. Protestants were then ordered to abjurate or leave. They left in great numbers, going first to Holland, Switzerland, England, and then to America. This deprived France of many of her most skilled artisans, the country being now forced into the blind policy of might, under the most un-Christian leadership of Rome, reaping thus some temporary glory on the battlefields, but at the expense of much misery to her people.

Meanwhile in the fields of religion, philosophy, and science, Giordano Bruno had appeared after Cardinal de Cusa. He brought before the Roman Church the theory of a limitless universe, associated with the great belief in Re-birth. To adopt such a viewpoint would have meant for Rome, to discard the theology created by St. Thomas Aquinas on the doubtful foundation given to the world by the Greek Aristotle in 350 B. C.; and would have led necessarily to the renewed belief in Reincarnation as of Christ and Origen.

The audacity of Bruno must be crushed! Unlike the prominent de Cusa he was not a powerful cardinal. The Inquisition threw him in a dungeon, but seven years of confinement could not make Bruno change his belief or yield to the threats of the Papacy. Finally, on February 17, 1600, he was burned at the stake as a heretic—Reincarnationist.

Like Christ, Bruno gave his life for the cause of Justice. He died in the flames leaving to history his memorable answer to his judges: "You fear to pass sentence on me more than I fear to receive it!" He displayed the serenity of spiritual conviction, the poise and control of the Reincarnationist. "Herein is the patience and faith of the saints." Like Christ he knew what manner of death awaited him and could have escaped his fate by yielding to his inquisitors; his dying words, as those of the Nazarene, demonstrated a great pity but no hatred.*

Meanwhile Protestantism was making further progress. Luther had denounced the exclusive right of the Roman hierarchy to interpret the Scriptures. He had gone so far as to announce: "The book that preaches Christ is apostolic, were its author Judas, Pilate, or Herod."

Where the Roman Church had claimed the divine privilege of formulating the spiritual thought of the people, Luther allowed them more freedom of thought. But his personal convictions were limited and controlled by his pronounced antipathy for all philosophy and mysticism. He ignored the Biblical teaching of Reincarnation, and in further error, instilled in the Reformist movement the subjugation and fear borrowed from the Catholic Church, teaching that men should bow and submit before religious authority.

However, this period of early Protestantism was not devoid of inspirational progress. Kepler, the astronomer and physicist, came into prominence at this time, advancing ideas of the universe in

---

* The death of Bruno is in many respects analogous to that of Joan of Arc, described in "Historical Proofs of Reincarnation," by the same authors.

accordance with those of Cardinal de Cusa and Giordano Bruno, i. e., Platonic and Pythagorean.

Confirming the illustrious Copernicus, Kepler gave another deadly blow to the Aristotlean-Church belief that the earth was the center of the universe. The imaginery spheres to which Aristotle had attached the stars, in his system of thought, were blown away as so many illusions of the past. The scientific foundation of the Roman Church was now proven to be as unstable as treacherous quicksands. There were danger signals as vivid as when a century before, Henry VIII had declared himself, in defiance to papal authority, the supreme power of the Church of England.

If Protestantism had then modified the narrow-minded attitude of Luther and recognized both Science and the complete teachings of Jesus, by admitting Reincarnation into its creed, the world would have been saved from much disaster, and the Roman Church might have been forced to accept the ancient belief or face destruction. But the Reformists themselves were lost in a maze of conflicting interpretations of the Scriptures, which they construed so literally and with so little spiritual insight, as to again lead to an era of persecution, particularly in Northern Europe, during which more stakes were erected than by the Roman Church, for the burning of so-called "heretics" and sorcerers, regardless of age or sex. A sad page in the history of Protestantism; a blind following of the edicts of the Jehovah of wrath and intolerance, thereby falling into the very error of the Catholic Church.

Early Protestantism could not understand a Reincarnationist like Kepler, any more than in the same days the Roman Church could understand the vision of Giordano Bruno. The great "Mystic," as he is sometimes called, suffered also from persecutions, but more fortunate than Bruno, he saw his scientific work recognized before his death in 1630.

Notwithstanding the appalling difficulties encountered in this period by Science, it could not be checked. The Italian Galileo, another great physicist and astronomer, completed the work of the German Kepler, together with the founding of a new scientific doctrine after his classic experiments from the Pisa Tower in 1591. The Inquisition did not spare him, and this may account for the fact that he prudently refrained from openly announcing himself as a Reincarnationist, remembering the fate of Bruno.

The Aristotlean theory was now destroyed; it was established that the sun was not revolving around the earth, which was no longer the center of the universe—a fearful shock to both Catholic and Protestant theologians who believed in the literal infallibility of the Bible. For instance, how could the miracle of Joshua be explained: "So the sun stood still in the midst of heaven and hasted not to go down about a whole day," if it was the earth that revolved around the sun?

During this same period, in 1596, the Frenchman Descartes was born: a great scientist and profound thinker. He was the founder of the Cartesian philosophy and also known as the father of modern philosophy; the first to propound the unitary law of the universe. As a modern Pythagoras in mathematics, he naturally admitted the pre-existence of the Soul. Yet he proceeded in his reasoning through a new process of doubt. Contrary to modern agnostics, he learned through this negative concept, which must be understood on its mathematical basis: no doubt, no investigation; no problem, no solution. Mathematics is the key to all solutions whether in keeping the expense account of the housewife, or in finding the fourth dimension of Einstein.

Descartes applied the Pythagorean principle to his philosophy through geometry, and his mathematical precision brought forth the principle, "I think, therefore I am," in a clearer way than the efforts of St. Augustine. He demonstrated the same cold precision in proving the existence of God, through a solution not far from the Platonic and Pythagorean concepts, just as in the same epoch the youthful Pascal obtained his wonderful "mystic hexagon" from a Pythagorean as well as Archimedean basis.*

Another great philosopher and scientist appeared in Germany—Leibnitz, born in 1646—an outstanding figure as a Reincarnationist, who soared like an eagle above the chaotic world conditions of his days following the Thirty Years' War. He had a definite belief in the pre-existence of the Soul, and while he conveyed this greatest of all beliefs in his native land, Ralph Cudworth, the famous English leader of thought, taught it in the British Isles. The resurrection indeed of true religion: Reincarnation linked with Science!

Many other great men of this period, taught the

---

* See "Historical Proofs of Reincarnation."

Re-birth principle, if not directly, at least indirectly. The theory of Will of Kant, for instance, cannot possibly be expressed better than by the Reincarnationist, who, following the example of Christ, carries his Will to the Cross, or the stake—like Bruno—if necessary. And beyond the grave—for a Will that ceases to function at the transition of death, is merely limited to the physical expression; but that which continues on its journey through incarnation after incarnation, is the Absolute and Divine Will that carries the Soul onward to the realization of the command and promise of Christ, "Be ye therefore perfect."

CHAPTER VI

SHIFTING SANDS

Civilization was moving westward. Having appealed to the "Supreme Judge of the World," America had proclaimed her independence. At one stroke a new page was written in the book of history; the Church had become an organization entirely independent of the State. The arbitrary teachings of both the Roman Church and the Protestants had forced thousands of people to emigrate from their native lands. A young nation was rising, which through its original belief in freedom of thought, was destined to become one of the greatest on earth.

Already Rome had been casting hungry eyes on the new and rich field. In 1789 an official representative was sent to America, and Baltimore was chosen as the first bishopric. Protestantism was already entrenched in the new land, but Rome knew it could rely on the result of its greater unity and discipline, and on what had already been accomplished in the South through missionaries following fast in the steps of Colomb. There was thus on one side of the new spiritual battlefield the stern figure of Puritanism, and on the other side the shadow projected from the Vatican, when suddenly there broke in Europe the fierce storm of the French Revolution.

Weary of a God of wrath, the French had clamored for Justice, and failing to receive it had taken the law into their own hands that they might live. The teachings of Voltaire, Rousseau, and other atheist philosophers of the day, were only a secondary cause of the tumult that rose in a fury never equalled except by the modern Russian Revolution.

On the debris of desecrated crosses from the profaned churches, the Goddess of Reason was raised up for public worship, not only in Paris, but, through French conquest, in Rome also. Pope Pius VI, then eighty-three years of age, was denied his request to be allowed to at least die in Rome. For a time it looked as if the Papacy itself was exterminated. Roman Christianity was abolished; it had failed through misinterpretation, intolerance, and injustice. And from the blood of protesting humanity was born the infamous Red Flag that waves to this day.

In the darkness of this religious night, the light of the brilliant Napoleon flashed forth. Like all great leaders he knew that religion is the mainstay of the people. Also his personal ambition was great. With Rome become French territory, the Church was feeling its way toward a recovery. Pope Pius VI had died a prisoner, but cleverly enough Bonaparte had seen that impressive funeral services were given him. The Roman Church saw in the Corsican general a means of salvation. A personal friend of his was ordained Pope under the name of Pius VII. Finally an agreement was reached with the atheist government of France.

The prediction of Lafayette, hero of the American Independence War was coming true. Bonaparte, still First Consul, was fast ascending towards the throne, and was to receive the imperial crown from the hands of the Pope. Also, he was to receive it in Paris, where atheism had ruled so recently in the shadow of the guillotine, from which had rolled the heads of Louis XVI and Queen Marie Antoinette into a basket of sawdust.

The accomplishment of this ambition was a victory both for Bonaparte and the Roman Church. But almost at once the struggle for supremacy started between the new Emperor and Rome. In May, 1809, Napoleon I, quoting the words of Christ, "My kingdom is not of this world," pub-

lished the famous decree which was a means of
withdrawing all temporal power from the Pope.
Like his predecessor, Pius VII was made a prisoner
and sent to France. Ambition had over-ruled
friendship!

Four years later, Napoleon realized his error, but
too late, when he was already defeated by the
Coalition headed by Protestant England. He had
dreamed of becoming a new Henry VIII, a spiritual leader as well as a conqueror. Yet, his domi-
nant spirit flaming into expression in such words
as "Minutes are everything—men are nothing!"
enabled him to conquer, and France paid the bitter
price in the blood of the flower of her manhood.

But Napoleon gained physical supremacy only;
in the spiritual realm he failed entirely, in spite
of his efforts to revive the old law of "divine
right" transmissible through heredity, and his
power to use men as pawns in the furthering of
his ambitious schemes. Between his method of at-
taining his purposes and the ideal of Justice,
yawned a tremendous gulf. "All that is of man
shall fail," and the light of the brief comet that had
blazed across the sky of Europe was suddenly extinguished. Once more the Roman Church breathed
freely, though still refusing to see the light.

From that period onward, the scientific belief
in Re-birth continued to shine forth; in Germany
particularly, where Schelling and his disciples renewed Neoplatonism through the "World-Soul"
idea. Schelling's theory of infinite progress could
not be tenable except through belief in Reincarnation. In Germany, Hegel, the father of logic,
conveyed through his philosophy the true impression of the martyr Giordano Bruno. Then followed Schopenhauer, and Goethe, whose agreement
with the great belief in re-birth was demonstrated
strongly enough to be recorded by such conserva-
tive authorities as the "Encyclopedia Britannica."
Thus the golden thread of Truth, gleaming in the
"Aeneid" of the early Roman poet Vergil, was
interwoven in the tapestry of the years.

During the nineteenth century, scientific development brought about the new evolutionary principles of Lamarck, Darwin, Spencer, and Haeckel,
which have created endless controversy. Here
again, we find that no better final expression can
be obtained than through the formula of re-birth.
Missing links—or links themselves—do not disturb
the Christian Reincarnationist; present or absent,
they do not interfere with the scientific foundation

of his belief, that does not even consider the Earth as the first vehicle.

Why argue so much about Evolution, when summing up the quarrels of the opponents, we find that the evolutionists declare man to evolve from animal form, and the Bible states that Adam was created from dust—or the mineral kingdom, not immediately, but through a long process equally as evolutionary, when reckoned in terms of time as given in the Bible.

While the evolutionary cult was gathering followers, Protestantism and Catholicism continued their fight, extending now the world over. Continuing to ignore Christ as the Reincarnationist, both were powerless to prevent in the early sixties, the fratricidal Civil War of America. Indeed, the sad days of Secession were only the logical result of the weak teachings of the Orthodox Churches. Had the great belief in Re-birth been taught instead of meaningless theological phraseology, prior to the coming of Abraham Lincoln, slavery would not have existed, such a condition being radically opposed to the Christian Reincarnationistic principle of Universal Justice, and much bloodshed would have been averted.

Christianity failed there once more to prevent

the addition of another frightful evidence of its misguidance to the pages of history. Since then the Franco-Prussian war of 1870-71 proved another striking example of its impotence.

Strangely enough, both France, by then again "the eldest daughter" of the Church, and the Roman Church itself, suffered terribly through that year 1870. France was defeated by Germany, and the Vatican lost once more "the kingdoms of the world and the glory of them" to the soldiers of Italy, inflamed by the words of Garibaldi.

Starting in true mediaeval fashion—through assassination—the great World War came in August, 1914, and the world again looked to Christianity in vain for relief and succor, Added to the holocaust of millions of innocent victims, there followed the horrors of the inevitable aftermath, from which the nations have not yet recovered. As one result of the ensuing world chaos, the Russian Revolution was precipitated; the Churches were openly defied, ridiculed, and destroyed.

At the present writing, misconstrued Christianity is powerless to prevent the uprising in the East. And with the echo of innumerable agonized voices scarcely hushed on the plains of Flanders, the threatening clouds of new and greater horrors loom on the purple horizon.

The nations are in a state of revolt and rebellion, dissatisfied with religious beliefs that lead only to war and destruction, instead of pointing the way to conquest of the elements, and of Self, to equality and Justice. Since the Russian Revolution we have seen Spain of Inquisition fame, and Mexico, cast off the yoke of religious dominion; in 1905 France had already issued her decree of separation of Church and State.

Yet in spite of its new-found religious freedom, the world is travailing in anxiety for the morrow. The past record of the Churches hold out no hope for peace or better world conditions in the future. More than ever man needs a religion to **live by**— not to die by—a belief that by its very essentials of Justice must needs influence and control him in his dealings with his fellow man. The Rock of spiritual vision on which Christ the Reincarnationist founded His Church, must be substituted for the shifting sands of man-made creeds and dogmas; then indeed it shall be true of resurrected Christianity: "The rain descended, and the floods came, and the winds blew and beat upon it, and it fell not, for it was founded on a Rock."

CHAPTER VII

THE BETTER DAWN

The Orthodox Churches have at no time lost sight of the fact that the number of their adherents is vastly exceeded by the millions of believers in Oriental Reincarnation. They have tried to make it appear that conditions arising from other sources, such as the deplorable caste system of India, and the opium traffic, etc., are to be attributed to this "pagan" belief. They have sent and still send their missionaries to convert the heathen to Christianity.

The false propaganda disseminated in general concerning the Re-birth belief, has led many people to the erroneous conclusion that Reincarnation is purely an Oriental conception that cannot be associated with Western thought. The attitude of the Theosophists has not helped to correct this false impression, especially as their principal leaders have tried to establish as a cold science what is in its essence a component part of the religion of Christianity. Furthermore, some of their leaders have admitted many childish absurdities which have thus become associated with the belief in Re-birth in the minds of many people.

CHRISTIANITY CRUCIFIED

The life of Christ far surpasses that of Buddha in many fundamental respects. The Reincarnationist belief cannot stand aloof from the complete teachings of Christ—it is a part of the Word. If the entire teachings of Christ had been conveyed from the beginning, as by Origen and other prominent Reincarnationists of the early Church, there is no doubt that the followers of Buddha would have been won over in large number to the **greater faith.***

If Buddhism is responsible for conditions in the Orient today, then Christianity is no less responsible for modern conditions in the Western World. We know these conditions in the far East, through personal experience and contact, and in toto they are no worse in many respects than conditions prevailing now in the heart of some of our fairest cities, where the people are living in direst poverty, and actually starving, while crime is rampant. And those who have heard that most horrible of sounds: the heart-rending cries and moans of soldiers dying in slow and terrible agony, crucified on the barbed wires stretched across "No Man's

---

* Buddhism makes unfounded claims as to exact length of incarnations, recollections, etc., and is merely a man-made philosophy. Christian Reincarnation is essentially a religion embodying true worship of God the Father.

Land" in the World War, will bear witness to the fact that nothing worse could ever happen in the Orient or elsewhere. What the Orient and the Western World need is the teaching of a complete and true Christianity embodying the great principle of Re-birth.

Another great objection to the belief in Reincarnation is the apparent lack of recollection of our previous lives, and none are so prone to raise this objection as those who are willing to accept so much on "faith" when connected with orthodox beliefs. Space does not permit us to go into this phase of the subject here; it is treated at length in another book.*

Men of science now enjoy more freedom than at any other period of the Christian era. It is not so long since chemistry was considered as a purely occult idea. But these learned men still cling to the fringes of this most ancient belief, consciously or unconsciously. A great French school founded by Allan Kardec definitely believes in Reincarnation; Gustave Geley and Camille Flammarion sustained the belief without question; in England Sir Oliver Lodge mentions it as a great possibility and falls into significant terminology in his recent book,

---

* See "Missing Links" by the authors.

"Man and the Universe": "Take our present incarnation, for instance . . ." The late Sir Conan Doyle made the statement, that "the balance of evidence shows that Reincarnation is a fact."

Many leading thinkers and scientists of the day agree that the only religion that can stand the test of the ages, is one embodying the findings of Science. A far cry from the utterance of St. Augustine: "Nothing is to be accepted save on the authority of the Scriptures, for greater is that authority than the powers of the human mind," and who then proceeded to claim infallibility of interpretation rather than of the Word itself.

Bergson's "Creative Evolution" in France, and William James' "Unity of Consciousness" in America—whether or not so intended by their creators—lead also necessarily to the thought of re-birth as the one indispensible means of establishing continuity. Why are we interested in the past? Primarily because we were associated with it; otherwise it would have but little value and interest for us—hardly more than yesterday's newspaper.

The Orthodox Churches have persisted in following the error of the Catholic Church in casting aside the teachings of Christ as a Reincarnationist. They naively admit spirits as existent, but not their re-embodiment. According to their belief, **God becomes the servant of man,** being compelled to create new Souls for the supply of physical bodies brought into existence according to the expression of man's physical desire—or through the deadly sin of "concupiscence"—so described by St. Augustine. If the Soul comes into being only at birth, how can it then be immortal? if it had a beginning it must have an end.

The issue remains the same between Catholicism and Protestantism as when the reformist movement commenced. The Catholic Church claims the right to interpret the Scriptures exclusively for its followers; each Protestant denomination determines its interpretation by the tenets of its own particular creeds and beliefs; the Unitarians reserve the right of individual interpretation, each man for himself. There is no true unity of thought; all reject the great **unifying** principle of re-birth, plainly indicated in the Scriptures. Those who claim belief in the infallibility of the Bible, appear to completely disregard the incontrovertible fact, stated previously in another chapter, that unless all four Gospels lie, Christ referred to John the

Baptist as a living example of this great truth, stating that he was the reincarnation of Elijah, the prophet of the Old Testament.

The Jews who certainly knew more about the Old Testament than any subsequent translator could possibly have known, were believers in Re-incarnation, as the Assyrians, Babylonians, Persians, and Hindus were before them. To deny the principle of re-birth as expressed in the words of Job, for instance: "Naked came I out of my mother's womb, and naked must I return thither," and the passages prophesying the reincarnation of Elijah, is equivalent to stating that the Jews knew less about their own tongue than modern theologians, which would constitute a gross absurdity.

In the last half century, Science has made more rapid strides than at any other period in history. Each new steps attests to the immortality of Soul. With the discovery that in its very essence, the atom—so long regarded as "dead matter"—is spiritual and immortal, tremendous possibilities confront us. The leading scientists look ahead to the day when atomic energy shall be released. What will be the result when this illimitable power is released in a world where might is still regarded as right?

CHRISTIANITY CRUCIFIED

"Yet what availeth man's increasing skill
The ever-broadening dominance of Will,
If increased wisdom walks not hand-in-hand,
Directing the vast power at his command?
The mighty forces at his will unleashed,
May turn and rend him, if not over-reached
By stern adherence to high spiritual laws
Decreeing that each motivated cause,
Shall bring its own immutable effect,
And that no power invoked can e'er protect
Man from the harvesting of self-sown seed,
From each full consequence of every deed."*

The only "safe and sane" scientific progress is that which keeps step with a religion rooted in Love, Truth, and Justice. With the growing conviction of the omniscience of spirit in the minds of scientists themselves, they realize that even if their experiments to produce life chemically or electrically are successful, they will be no nearer the true solution of the mystery of life. The Creator ever looms before us as infinitely greater than His creation.

Professor Sheldon, head of the Department of Physics of New York University, stated recently

---

* "How Can God Be Love" by Marguerite Beighton Pless, author of "October Days," "Literary Digest," November, 1930, and other poems.

according to the newspapers, that there was no reason why eventually we would not be able to control such natural laws as that of gravity, which among other things would enable us to step out from the window and walk through the air as safely as we now do on terra firma. Incidentally he has stated that we are analagous to the sounds produced when a chord of music is struck or a musical instrument is played—an exact Pythagorean conception of universal harmony.

Many years before the airplane came into existence, Tennyson, the prophetic poet, foretold its use in war activities, and the creating of a World League.

> "And there rained a ghastly dew,
> From the nations' airy navies,
> Grappling in the central blue . . .
> Til the war-drums throbbed no longer,
> And the battle flags were furled
> In the Parliament of Man,
> The Federation of the World."

Yet the League of Nations is failing at this writing in its primary object of establishing peace on earth. Why? It is composed of intellectual men, who cannot in their hearts accept the religion of today, and who realize that it is powerless to prevent further war or to cope with the problems of the teeming multitudes. Their hearts fail them as history threatens to repeat itself in more horrible bloodshed and destruction. There is no true unity among them or the nations that they represent.

The people have asked for bread and have been given a stone; they have asked for Justice and swords have been offered them. They see the miracle of re-incarnating life all around them; they witness the ugly worm emerge from the chrysalis a glorious butterfly. Their spirits grope towards "the larger hope."

But they are told this magic of transformation is not for them; that of all God's creatures they are the most wretched, being born in sin, from which there is no escape except through abject belief in an angry God who must be continually importuned, lest they be punished through all eternity for "the deeds done in the body" during one short span of years on earth.

The people can rise no higher than their ideals. Taught to worship an unjust God, how can they hope to manifest or receive anything but injustice? And so long as injustice prevails, there will be poverty breeding crime and revolt; there will be "wars and rumors of wars."

"Without vision the people perish." The deepest human need is the ever-broadening spiritual vision of the just and loving God revealed by Christ, the vision translating life into terms of glorious opportunity, instead of a painful period of struggle and suspense that determines the eternal verdict of the dread hereafter.

Liberty, Equality, and Justice will be attained only by following the true teachings of Christ; only thus will Peace be assured on earth.

Sin and crime will continue unabated until combated with spiritual education and enlightenment, rather than human vengeance, for man cannot mete out just retribution.

Only with the correct spiritual education from infancy will the problems of "flaming youth" be solved. Taught to regard their bodies as "temples of God" and themselves as "sons of God" they will not be likely to profane their high heritage of divinity. And the saying is trite but true, that "the youth of today are the citizens of tomorrow."

In the World Church, founded on the rock of Christian Reincarnation, united in worship of God the Father, with the inspiration and example of Christ ever shining before His followers, they will

"press forward to the mark of their high calling"—
the perfection taught by Him. The true Brotherhood of "one fold and one shepherd" will be
achieved at last under the banner of Christ the
Reincarnationist; a new Te Deum of praise and
thanksgiving will be sung on earth.

"Despair's long night is o'er, and Hope with starry
    eyes
 Looks where the hand of God writes JUSTICE
    in the skies;
Along the sweep of life a fairer day is born,
 And rose-flung into space, there shines the Better
    Dawn."

THE END

APPENDIX

It is impossible to condense a complete record of religious history in the space of this small volume. For the benefit of such readers as may be interested the following brief summary is added.

According to the Jewish reckoning based on the Old Testament record of creation, the beginning of the World is estimated as dating back to only 3761 B. C. The Jews ceased to exist as a nation forty years after the death of Christ, being dispersed by the Romans and thereafter known as the "scattered kingdom." The enigma of their survival after world-wide persecution is explained only through the law of Reincarnation.

Mohammedism or Islamism was created by Mohammed in 622 in the temple of Kaaba near Mecca, Arabia. It is based on the concept of God akin to the Jewish delineation: "Koran, Tribute, or Sword!" Today is still holds sway over many millions in Africa, Asia, and Europe.

In the western world, together with the Albigenses, the forerunners of Protestantism were the Waldenses, who rose in France under Peter Waldo in 1168. They also were terribly persecuted until the 17th century when Cromwell and the Protestant nations acted in their defense.

From the great Protestant sects of Lutherism, Calvinism, and the Church of England many denominations branched off, among which were the Scotch Episcopaleans in the 16th century, through separation from the Church of England; the Presbyterians, Calvinistic and Trinitarian in doctrine. The latter established themselves in America in 1640, combining Calvinistic and Arminian teachings. The Baptists, Calvinistic as a whole, organized in 1639 in Providence, R. I., under Roger William, as American Baptists, now subdivided into many sects with varying creeds. The Methodists who were first organized in England by the Wesleys in 1729, left Calvinism to adhere to the Arminian doctrine—the five articles of faith established by J. Arminius of Holland in the 16th century, constituting the foundation of American Methodist theology.

The Unitarians, who deny the Trinity, organized in more recent years; also the Universalists following a doctrine which is a modification of Presbyterianism. Perhaps unconsciously the Unitarians share in the Pythagorean principle of Unity, while the Universalists follow the Pythagorean principle of Harmony through their expression of the final harmony attained by all Souls with God.

In America, Lutherism branched off into five sub-denominations, and there also the Friends or Quakers became strongly organized in the 18th century. The many other subdivisions of Protestantism existing today are too numerous to mention.

Subsequently, the following independent bodies came into existence in America: The Church of Jesus Christ of Latter Day Saints or Mormons, in 1830, and the Christian Science Church in 1866.

CPSIA information can be obtained
at www.ICGtesting.com
Printed in the USA
BVOW07s1739250917

495851BV00009B/77/P